What shall we say to God today?

**Prayers to use
with young children**

Edited by Helen Albans

NCEC

Acknowledgements

CONTRIBUTORS

Helen Albans
David Cavil
Roy Chapman
Jose Finlayson
Catherine Guy
Valerie Ogden
Simon Oxley
Hazel Snashall
Peter Tongeman
Gillian Weeks

Edited by Helen Albans
Cover design by Image-On Artworks

Published by:
National Christian Education Council
1020 Bristol Road
Selly Oak
Birmingham
B29 6LB

British Library Cataloguing-in-Publication Data:
A catalogue record for this book is available from the British Library.

ISBN 0-7197-0922-9

First published in 1985 as *When you pray with 3-6s*
Second edition 1998
© 1985, 1998 National Christian Education Council

Designed and typeset by National Christian Education Council

Printed and bound by Biddles Limited, Guildford

Contents

Foreword

The prayers in this collection are intended for use with young children aged from three to six.

They are rooted in the everyday experience of young children, and attempt to put those experiences into words and to make connections between everyday life and the teachings of Jesus in ways likely to make sense to children.

In many cases, suggestions are made about topics for discussion which can lead naturally into the prayer. In many, too, there is scope for incorporating the children's own suggestions. Some prayers have simple responses – these are printed in bold type for easy identification.

The prayers are arranged into themes, making it quick and easy to find prayers on particular topics.

Prayer has many facets, and speaking prayers out loud is only one way of praying. Over a period of time, it is good if children are introduced to other ways – using silence, movement and meditation for example. This collection of prayers is offered as a resource to dip into when words are required, in the hope that it may prove useful.

God:
Loving Creator

The natural world

1   Lord, what a great big world you have made:
towering mountains,
deep oceans,
the high blue sky,
and vast forests and deserts.
You have painted the world with beautiful, bright colours.
You have made it all.
You look after it all.
Lord, how wonderful you are!

2   Loving God,
you made the daytime for us to work and play;
you made the night for us to sleep and rest.
You never sleep.
You watch over us and care for us, day and night,
always.
Thank you, loving God.

3   Creator God, we look up at your great sky,
and we praise you.
For the sun which gives us warmth and light,
we praise you.

For the moon, first a silver crescent then a great white ball,
we praise you.
For the stars, like twinkling lights in the dark sky,
we praise you.
For the people who study the sky and show us how really great you are,
we praise you.

4

Lord God,
you made the high snow-capped mountains
and the rolling green and purple hill.
You made the streams, running down like silver ribbons,
growing into rivers which race over the pebbles and
crawl through the deep places, to mingle with the water
of the sea and the waves, lapping the beach.
Thank you, Lord God, for your beautiful world.

5

Thank you, God,
for the gentle breeze,
cooling us on hot summer days;
for the playful wind,
tossing the heads of the flowers;
and for the strong wind,
making whirlpools of dancing autumn leaves.
Take care of the people who have to be outside and at sea
in howling gales. Keep them safe, Lord God.

Plants, flowers and vegetables

6

For the flowers of many colours which brighten up our world:
We thank you, loving God.
For the crocuses and hyacinths and flowers which grow indoors:
We thank you, loving God.
For pansies, lupins and lilies in our gardens:
We thank you, loving God.
For roses, marigolds and wallflowers in the park:
We thank you, loving God.

For snowdrops, primroses and bluebells in the woods:
We thank you, loving God.
For dandelions, buttercups and poppies in the fields:
We thank you, loving God.

7 *Let the children see and touch some seeds and bulbs as an introduction to this prayer. Explain that small, brown seeds and dull, dry bulbs are really flowers asleep, waiting for the spring sunshine to wake them up.*

How wonderful it is that when the cold sleep of winter is over, you bring seeds and bulbs to life and make beautiful flowers grow from them. For the miracle of new life we praise you, Creator God.

8 *Ask the children for suggestions of fruit and vegetables to include in this prayer.*

Creator God, thank you for vegetables and fruits.
You give us potatoes, carrots, beans and peas.
You give us apples, oranges, grapes and bananas.
Help us not to be greedy, but to share your good gifts with others.

9 When we see the tall trees swaying in the wind,
and the colourful autumn leaves falling
to make a carpet in the woods;
when we sit in the cool shade of the oak or chestnut tree,
or hear the breeze whispering through the first treetops;
We want to praise and thank you, God, for your beautiful world.

Birds and animals

10 The blackbird calls us from our bed,
while cheeky sparrows peck at bread;
the blue-tits play at acrobats,
and song-thrush cheers us with his notes;
the swallow swoops past, flying low,
and friendly robin chirps, 'Hello!'

No wonder Jesus loved the birds,
and often told us in his words,
they're always in God's love and care,
like us, and people everywhere.

11 Dear God, you made the animals:
the graceful horses with their foals,
the elephant and kangaroo,
the wolf, the bear and lion too.
You gave the farmer useful friends
like pigs and cows and goats and sheep;
and for our friends you gave us pets:
the rabbits, dogs and cats we keep.
Perhaps, God, when they bark and squeak
they're really trying hard to speak
a thank-you prayer, which we pray too:
'You made us, God, and we thank you.'

12 Lord, you made so many different insects:
humming bees and clicking grasshoppers,
dragon-flies with rainbow wings,
spiders, ants and centipedes,
gnats and moths and butterflies,
scurrying beetles and other creepy things.
You care about them all!
How kind you are!
Thank you, Lord.

People

13 Thank you, Lord, for babies:
for chicks gathered under the hen's wings,
for lambs skipping in the fields,
for kittens and puppies in our homes,
and especially for our baby brothers and sisters.
Help mothers and fathers everywhere to look after their
     babies well.

14 Lord God, we belong to a great family of millions of people from all countries of the world. We have different kinds of faces, different coloured skins, and we are all different shapes and sizes! Yet, Lord, you know everyone in your world family. Thank you, Lord, for loving them all.
Thank you, Lord, for loving me.

15 *Speak the prayer slowly, allowing time for the children to make relevant movements with their hands.*
Lord, we look at our hands,
we look at each finger and thumb.
We can spread them out like fans,
and push with them, and pull, and drum.
Our fingers wiggle, run and shake,
never stopping while we're awake.
Lord, with our hands we work and play,
let them be used for you today.

Looking after God's creation

16 Creator God, lots of people help you to make the things
we need.
You made the corn which grows in the fields,
and people grind it into flour
and bake bread for us to eat.
You made the sheep,
and people clip and clean the wool
and make it into warm clothes for us to wear.
Thank you for letting people share with you in making
things.

17 Creator God, you made a world full of beautiful and useful things, and you want us to help look after them. We are sorry that people spoil your world by carelessly throwing away rubbish, and by wasting the food and water that other people need. Help us to be unselfish and to look after your world well.

God: Loving Creator

God our loving parent

18 Lord Jesus, when you talked to God you called him
'Father' and you told us he is our heavenly Father too.
Thank you for showing us how kind and loving God is,
caring about us and helping us, just like the best Dad in
the whole world.

19 Lord God, our mums and dads show us how much they
love us
by giving us the things we need,
by forgiving us when we are sorry for doing wrong,
by being interested in everything which happens to us.
You are like that, too. You are our heavenly Father and
Mother.
Thank you for loving us.

20 Lord God, Jesus told us how much you care for the world;
you give food for the birds,
you look after the flowers in the fields,
you give us the things we need which are good for us,
you are like a loving parent.
You know what is best for us.
We thank you and ask that everybody in the world may
have the things they need to make them happy.

21 Thank you, loving God, for people who help us with hard
and difficult things.
Thank you for helping us too. When we feel lonely, or sad,
or have difficult things to do, you are with us to help us,
because we are your children.

22 Thank you, God, for our mums and dads, aunties, uncles,
grannies and grandads.
They help us learn how to draw and write, to bake cakes
and grow seeds in the garden.
Thank you, God, that you help us to learn – through your
Spirit inside us, through other people and through the
Bible.

23 Sometimes if we are frightened we need someone to cuddle us or hold our hand. Help us to remember, God, that when we are afraid you are with us too. Although we cannot see you we know that you promised to be near us and to keep us safe. You always keep your promises. Thank you, loving God.

24 *To follow the reading of the parable of the lost son, in Luke 15.*
Lord Jesus, you told the story about a father whose son ran away from home. The father never stopped loving that son. He was always waiting for him to come back. You told us that God is like that father. He never stops loving us. Help us to love him too.

Jesus Christ

Advent, birth and childhood

Getting ready for Christmas

TRINITY 29-11-15

25 Lord God, we read in the Bible about how different people
got ready for Jesus to be born.
There was an angel who told Mary about her baby;
and Joseph who made sure that Mary had a safe journey
  to Bethlehem;
and the wise men who followed a star to find the place
  where Jesus was born.
Thank you for everyone who got ready to welcome Jesus.
Help us to get ready too.

26 *Prayers to use week by week when lighting candles on an
Advent ring. Repeat the first two lines, using the ending
for the appropriate week, before lighting each candle.*

Light a candle – watch it glow,
shining bright so we may know about...

Week one: The prophets
Thank you, God, for the prophets, people who lived a
long time before Jesus was born, but who told
everybody that one day a special king would come.
Jesus the King is coming!
Hurray!

Week two: Mother Mary

Thank you, God, for Mary, Jesus' mother, who gave birth to him in a stable, who loved him and looked after him until he was grown up.
Jesus the King is coming!
Hurray!

Week three: John the Baptist

Thank you, God, for John the Baptist who shouted out, 'Prepare the way of the Lord!' John helped people to get ready to meet Jesus by baptizing them in the River Jordan.
Jesus the King is coming!
Hurray!

Week four: God's people

Thank you, God, for making your people like one big family. Help us to remember that people all over the world will be celebrating Christmas, just like us, and saying 'Thank you' for the gift of Jesus.
Jesus the King is coming!
Hallelujah!

27 *To use when opening the windows on an Advent calendar.*

Another window to open,
another picture to look at,
another day nearer to Christmas.
It's fun to open our Advent calendars,
and the more windows we open, the more excited we feel.
Help us to remember, Lord, as we look at the pictures,
that we are getting ready for something very special:
not just for giving and receiving presents,
not just for special food and parties,
but for Jesus' birthday.
Help us to remember that.

28 We are learning some new carols,
putting up decorations,
making cards,

practising our nativity play...
(add more suggestions from the children).
We are enjoying all these special and exciting things, God.
We hope you like them too.

29

Thank you, God, for Christmas surprises:
for lumpy, bumpy stockings stuffed to the toe,
for brightly wrapped parcels with secrets inside,
for exploding crackers with hats and jokes.
Thank you for all the things that make us feel happy and
    excited at Christmas time.

30

Happy Christmas, everyone!
Thank you, Lord, for all the people we see at Christmas
    time:
people who are happy because they remember that Jesus
    was born.
Thank you for the friends we go to see, and the ones who
    come to see us, and the ones we can talk to on the
    telephone.
Please help all the people we know to have a happy
    Christmas.

31

When Jesus was born,
    a sparkling star shone in the sky.
When Jesus was born,
    people hurried to the stable to see him.
When Jesus was born,
    God gave the world a very special gift,
    the gift of love.
Help us, Lord, to give each other
    the gift of love this Christmas.

32

Thank you for Christmas music, Lord, for carols about
angels and shepherds and wise men and baby Jesus. We
like singing together to praise you, to thank you, and to
show that we feel happy because it's Christmas.

33 Loving God, we have been very busy practising our play
(or song, or service... as appropriate).
Thank you for our colourful costumes.
Thank you for the people *(add names)* who have helped us
to get ready.
Most of all, thank you for the wonderful story of how Jesus
was born.
We love the story, and we hope that through our acting
and singing other people will love it too.

34 Our church is a happy church today!
People are calling out, 'Happy Christmas!'
Children are showing each other their presents.
We are singing carols that we love,
and thanking God in our prayers for Jesus.
Thank you, God, that we are especially happy in church
today.

35 *Dedication*
Loving God,
we remember how Mary and Joseph took Jesus
to the temple church when he was a baby.
They promised to look after him.
The old people there welcomed him.
They were glad to see the special baby
they had been hoping for.
Thank you for all new babies,
for families who look after them,
for churches that welcome them,
and for all the happiness they bring.

Jesus the child

36 *Invite the children to mime appropriate actions as the
prayer is introduced.*
Let's think about the home Jesus lived in.
There's Mary sweeping the dusty floor:
swish, swish, swish!

There's Joseph busy hammering nails:
  bang, bang, bang!
There's Mary kneading the bread dough:
  thump, thumb, thump!
There's Joseph throwing twigs on the fire:
  crackle, crackle, crackle!
Lord, it's fun to imagine Jesus in a busy home where there
  were lots of jobs to do.
It's fun to imagine him helping his parents:
learning to sweep, and bake, and hammer, and light fires.
When there are jobs to be done on our homes may we
  watch, learn and help whenever we can.

37 When Jesus went to school he took off his shoes and sat
on the floor and listened to his teacher.
  He learned to read,
  he learned to pray,
  he learned to write.
Thank you for all the places where we learn – at home and
  church, at school, nursery or playgroup.
Thank you for all the ways we learn – talking and listening,
  reading and writing, painting, making things and
  playing.
Lord Jesus, we are glad to know what it is like to learn.

38 As we pray, let us remember that Jesus prayed too: at
home, and in the synagogue church. Jesus learned a
special prayer reminding him that God is great and
wonderful. The prayer said:
  'Hear, 0 Israel: The Lord our God is one Lord.'
God, we love you, as Jesus did, because you are great
and wonderful. Thank you that we can say our prayers and
know that you listen.

39 Jesus and his friends played lots of different games. They
loved to be in the fresh air, running and shouting and
playing:
  'Coming out to play, Jesus?'

'What shall we do?'

'Shall we kick a ball around, or play houses, or have a
race, or play at weddings and funerals?'

Thank you, loving God, for all the fun we have when we
play games with our friends:

outdoor games like football and hide-and-seek,

indoor games like board games or video games.

Thank you for all the different games we have, and the fun
of playing together.

40 Let's think about Jesus and his family. They had quiet
times together when they prayed to God; noisy times when
they went on outings; exciting times of special meals and
special festivals; sad times, when someone had been
naughty, or someone was ill.

Thank you for families, Lord:

for families who love us very much, whatever happens.

Help our families to be happy ones.

Friend, teacher and healer

Jesus the friend

41 Jesus was friends with so many people:
people who were ill,
people who were sad,
people who were happy,
mums and dads and children.

Jesus is our friend too.

He helps us to be friends with each other.

He teaches us to love and help one another.

Thank you, God, for the friendship of Jesus.

42 Thank you, Jesus, for being my friend. I know that you
listen when I talk to you, and you help me when I need
help, because that is what friends are for.

43 Loving God, we are glad that all over the world there are people who call themselves your friends.
Let the friendship of Jesus hold your world together in love and peace, helping us all to be friends with each other.

44 Jesus, we enjoy playing with the *(sand tray, water, etc)*.
Thank you for the fun we have playing together with our friends.

45 The disciples were friends of Jesus – Peter and Andrew, James and John and the others.
Mary and Martha were friends of Jesus – they welcomed him into their home.
Zacchaeus was a friend of Jesus – he was sorry that he had hurt people and promised that he would not do it again.
Hearing about all these people helps us to know Jesus.
We learn that he wants us to be his friends.
Thank you, God, for Jesus our friend.

46 Lord Jesus, sometimes we are very happy, sometimes we are very sad.
Lord Jesus, help us to share our happiness with you by sharing it with others;
when we are sad we will tell you about it so that you can share that too.

47 Lord Jesus, thank you for our friends.
Help us to be good friends and help us to make friends again if we quarrel.
May we never spoil our friendships by being selfish or always wanting our own way.
Help us to follow your example of love and kindness, always.

Jesus Christ: Friend, teacher and healer

48 Jesus had lots of friends:
Hurray!
We have lots of friends:
Hurray!
It's great to have friends:
Hurray!

Jesus the teacher

49 'Look at the flowers of the field; see how beautiful they
are,' said Jesus.
'Look at the birds,' said Jesus, 'God cares for them, and he
cares for you much more than flowers or birds.'
We know that you care for us, God, because Jesus has
told us so.
Thank you, God, for all your love and care.

50 Lord Jesus, Mary and Joseph looked after you and loved
you when you were a little boy at home. We are glad that
you have told us that God looks after us and loves us in
the same way.

51 Jesus, you have taught us to say our prayers to God; to
call him 'Father', to ask for his love and care, and to ask for
his forgiveness when we have done wrong.
Thank you, Jesus, for helping us to say our prayers.
(Now say together the prayer that Jesus taught.)

52 Loving God,
sometimes we hurt people:
we say words or do things that hurt them.
Jesus tells us that when we are sorry, you forgive us:
we are sorry; please forgive us and help us not to be
hurtful again.

53 Loving God, we enjoy finding out more about Jesus.
Thank you for those who help us to know him: our families,
our teachers and all our friends at church.

54 Jesus was always helping people who were ill or sad or
lonely.
Lord Jesus, be with your people today who need your help
and your care. Help us to show your love and care to
others.

55 Jesus says, 'Come and follow me'.
That means learning about him and then being the
loving sort of person he was.
Lord Jesus, may I know you more,
   love you more,
   and be more like you,
   every day.

56 For those who teach us about Jesus,
for those who tell us his stories,
for those who help us with music
to sing our songs of praise,
for all those who share with us at church,
thank you, loving God.

Stories of Jesus: prayers to be used before or after readings from the Gospels

57 Loving God, thank you for the Bible, which tells us the
story of Jesus. We are going to listen to a story about him
now.
(Read or tell a story about Jesus.)
Loving God, thank you for the story about Jesus. Help us
to be more like him every day.

58
We are glad that the Samaritan helped the wounded man.
He was brave and good to do that.
When there is anyone needing help,Lord Jesus, may we
be like the good Samaritan and do what we can to help.

59
Loving God, when we are lost, not sure where we are, or
where our friends or family are, we become frightened.
Jesus told a story about a sheep that was lost. Perhaps it
was frightened until the shepherd found it again, and then
it felt safe.
Thank you for those who look after us and make sure we
are safe. Jesus tells us that you care for us like the
shepherd cares for the sheep. We are glad about that.
Thank you, God!

60
Loving God, Jesus tells us that, like the father in the story,
you welcome us and love us when we come to you. Thank
you for showing us this.
We remember that in the story the older brother was not
welcoming. Help us to be ready to welcome everyone who
joins us here at church, and to be friends with them.

61
Lights shine out in the darkness:
street lights help us to walk safely,
lights in our homes help us to live in comfort.
'You have to be like lights,' said Jesus.
Lord Jesus, let our lives be like lights that help others for
your sake.

62
A little pinch of salt on crisps,
a shake of salt on fish and chips... Mmm!
'You have to be like the salt,' said Jesus, 'to make the
world better for everyone.'
Yes, Jesus, we will do that for you.

63 Jesus, it is exciting to hear stories about finding treasure – gold and jewels and pearls.
You teach us that the best treasure of all is belonging to you. Help us to have this best-of-all treasure.

64 Just a tiny seed and it grows into a big tree.
Jesus, you started out with just a few friends, and now you have people who love you and follow you all round the world.
The tree of your friends is still growing, and we are part of it today. Thank you, Jesus.

65 Jesus said that a tiny seed can grow into a big tree.
A tiny bit of love can make lots of people happy.
Take my love and make it grow, Lord Jesus, to make others happy.

66 Jesus, you said, 'Let the children come to me.'
Here we are, Jesus, ready to sing our songs of praise to you.
We are glad to come to you and glad to know you welcome us.

67 Loving God, we remember that Jesus showed love to everybody, whoever they were and whatever they were like. Please help us to learn to love as Jesus loved.

Jesus the healer

68 Helping people, healing people, and loving people:
every day you showed that you cared, Jesus.
You want people to care for each other.
Help us, Jesus, to do that.

69 Thank you, Jesus, for healing people when you were here on earth.
Please help those who look after sick people today.

70

Lord Jesus, be with those who are ill today.
May they know that we are thinking of them, and wanting
them to be well again.

71

When people who were ill went to Jesus, he helped them.
Loving God, we remember today people who are ill:
.... is at home.
.... is in hospital.
(Name people known to the children.)
Let the love of Jesus be round about them,
helping them to know they are not alone,
helping them to get well again.

72

Loving God, thank you that we do not have to be able to
see to enjoy the world you have made.
Thank you for the different things we can hear...
(Pause and let the children identify any sounds.)
Thank you for the different ways that blind people can find
things out using their ears and their fingers to help them.

73

Thank you, God, for the special dogs who work with blind
people, helping them to get around easily, even in busy
cities.
Thank you for the people who train them to be so useful.

74

Loving God, we know not everyone can hear easily.
Thank you for sign language and lip-reading and hearing
aids.

75

Lord Jesus, some people are deaf and cannot hear at all;
others cannot hear very well.
May we be kind and patient and thoughtful with those who
cannot hear us, and find other ways of communicating with
them.

76 Jesus, our Lord, you loved children and they came to you for a blessing. Be very near to children who are in hospital today. Bless them with health and healing that they may return home soon.

77 We ask you, Jesus, to bless children who have to stay in bed because they are ill. Let them soon be made well again.

78 Loving God, sometimes it seems as if everyone else finds things easy and we are the only ones struggling to do something.
Help us to remember that most people find some things difficult.
Help us to ask for help if we need it.
Help us to keep on trying and to find new ways of doing things that work for us.

79 Loving God, we thank you for:
    walking sticks and walking frames,
    wheelchairs and ramps for them to go up.
    (Mention people the children know who use these things.)
Thank you for all the things that make it easier for some people to get around.

80 When we can see and hear, walk and run, climb and play, help us, Lord, never to be unkind or uncaring for those who cannot do these things.

81 When we are ill we need people to care for us.
Thank you, God, for mums and dads, for doctors and nurses, health visitors and physiotherapists. Thank you for the care they give us to make us well again.

82 Loving God, bless those who are working hard in our hospitals today. All through the day and night, they care for people who are ill. We thank you for them.

Lord and King

Palm Sunday

83 *Look together at pictures of processions, carnivals and parades, and talk about them.*
Thank you, God, for processions:
adults and children, standing and watching;
brightly coloured lorries with people waving;
bands marching by, and clowns falling over;
balloons and badges, and buckets for pennies.
Thank you, God, for Jesus,
riding a donkey, while children waved branches,
shouting 'Hurray' as he went by.

84 Lord Jesus, you rode on a borrowed donkey.
All the people shouted, **Hurray for Jesus.**
Coats and leafy branches made a carpet for you.
All the people shouted, **Hurray for Jesus.**
We want to join in and say how much we love you,
so we all shout, **Hurray for Jesus.**

The Last Supper

85 *Talk together about special meals and parties, and adapt the first part of the prayer to reflect the children's experiences.*
Thank you, God, for special meals:
sausage and beans, jelly and ice cream,
eaten with our friends and family.
Thank you for Jesus, sitting with his friends,
eating a special meal to say 'Goodbye'.
Thank you that people still think of Jesus
by sharing a special meal of bread and wine.

Good Friday

86

Jesus, sometimes we call out,
  'Someone kicked me!'
  'Someone punched me!'
  'Someone pushed me over!'
We cry because it hurts.

Jesus, your mother and your friends cried
  when they saw you being hurt.
Jesus, you are always with us
  when we cry because it hurts.

Easter Sunday

87

We are alive today!
Jesus is alive today!
  Thank you, God.

88

This prayer should follow news-time. The first two parts of the prayer should be adapted accordingly.
Good news: the sun is shining.
Good news: our bulbs are flowering.
  Thank you, God, for good news.
Good news: Helen's gran has come to stay.
Good news: David's got new shoes.
  Thank you, God, for good news.
Good news: hot cross buns and Easter eggs.
Good news: happy Easter songs.
  Thank you, God, for good news.
Good news: Jesus is alive today.
Good news: Jesus is our friend.
  Thank you, God, for good news.

89

Talk with the children about times when they have felt sad because something went wrong; and then when they felt happy because the wrong thing was put right again.
Loving God,
when the friends of Jesus knew that he had died,
they thought that they had lost him.

They felt sad.
Then, on Easter morning, there he was!
They felt happy again.
May we share their happiness this Easter morning.

90 *Suitable for use following the retelling of the Easter story from John 20.1-18.*

Lord Jesus,
people who love us give us nice surprises:
    a surprise present,
    a surprise treat,
    a surprise hug and kiss.
You gave Mary a nice surprise:
    she thought that she was talking to the gardener
    and found that it was you!
You loved your friends then.
Thank you for loving us today.

91 Lord Jesus,
you are King
and you love us.
Help us to love you.

92 Loving God, following Jesus isn't always easy. We know he
wants us to be peaceful and kind and to think about
others, but sometimes we don't feel like doing any of those
things. When we feel that way, help us to make a special
effort to live as Jesus taught us to live.

93 *This prayer is more suitable for the upper end of the age-range. Talk about palaces: large buildings with guards outside and servants inside.*

Thank you, God, for Jesus the King.
    Jesus has no palace; he lives with us.
    Jesus has no guards to keep us out.
    Jesus has no servants, except us.
Thank you, God, for Jesus the King.

The Bible
and other books

The Bible

94

Let the children look at and handle a modern version of the Bible. Show them how much was written about the time before Jesus was born (the Old Testament), and how much was written about Jesus and his followers (the New Testament). Use parts of this prayer as appropriate.

Loving God,
we have discovered that the Bible is not just one book,
but a whole library of books.
For the many different kinds of writing in the Bible,
we thank you, loving God.

For those who wrote the Bible long ago,
in another language, with words we cannot understand,
and for those who translated it into our language,
so that we can understand it today,
we thank you, loving God.

For the people who printed the Bible words on paper,
for the people who gathered the paper into books,
for the people who drew pictures for us to enjoy,
we thank you, loving God.

Whenever we read the Bible, or look at its pictures, help us
to learn a little more about you.

95
Loving God,
we are glad there are so many stories about Jesus:
 when he was a baby in Bethlehem,
 when he was a boy, living with his family in Nazareth,
 when he was a man, helping and loving people.
Thank you, loving God, for all the stories about Jesus.

96
Thank you, loving God, for the stories about Jesus in the Bible.
The Bible tells us that when Jesus grew up, he told people how much God loves them, he healed those who were ill, and he helped those who were sad and lonely.
Thank you for the story of how, although cruel men killed him, Jesus came back again to show that death is not the end.

97
In the lines 'kings ... writers', add the names of biblical characters known to the children.

Loving God,
the Bible tells us about many important people:
 kings and queens,
 soldiers and shepherds,
 builders and teachers,
 fishermen and writers.
Some were old and some were young.
They were all important because they listened to you, and
 they did what you wanted them to.
We are glad, God, that you love all sorts of people and ask
 them to help you.

98
We praise you, God, that we can read in the Bible the story of the beginning of the Church.
We praise you
for great leaders: Peter, Paul, James and John,
 (add others known to the children)
for missionaries who travelled around the world,
 telling people about Jesus;
for churches that began in faraway places;

for people who learned to love and follow Jesus.
We thank you for martyrs who gave their lives for Jesus,
for your Spirit who made them brave and strong.

Other books

99 *Talk with the children about their favourite books and stories, and the characters in them. Incorporate their suggestions into the prayer.*

Loving God, we have talked about the books and stories
we enjoy. Some of our favourites are...
Thank you that there are so many different kinds of books:
  books about things that really happened...
  books of made-up stories...
  books full of pictures...
  books full of poems...
  books full of information... and many, many more.
Thank you, God, for a world full of books!

100 Dear Lord God,
thank you for adventure stories
  about children who do exciting things
    and visit strange places,
  about people who do hard or dangerous things
    in faraway countries.
You help people to do hard things, and to do them well.
Please help us when we have to do hard things, and make
  our lives adventurous too.

101 We like picture books, Lord:
  coloured pictures, and photographs;
  pictures of people and places;
  pictures of animals and birds;
  (add other items, as appropriate to the occasion)
  pictures that pop up as you open the page;
  pictures to copy or colour.
Thank you, Lord, for picture books.

102 We are learning to read and write, Lord – first the letters of our own names, and the names of our friends and family, then more and more words every day. Thank you that we can learn to read and write and that there are so many wonderful books for us to enjoy.

103 *Ask the children if they have bedtime stories read to them by a parent or other adult.*

Dear loving God, we like bedtime stories.
It is lovely to snuggle in bed and listen to a story. We shut our eyes and think about what is being read. When the story is finished, we have a goodnight kiss, and go to sleep. We feel happy and comfortable.
Thank you, loving God, for bedtime stories.

104 What a lot of books there are!
Some are picture books,
some have pictures and words,
and some have only words.
Help me to take care of all books,
and to treasure them,
so that other people can enjoy them too.

105 Thank you, God, for the library, where there are thousands of books for people to borrow.
Thank you for the people who look after all the books and make sure they are in the right places on the shelves.
May everyone who uses the library enjoy the books they borrow, and return them safely.

106 Loving God,
there are lots of things I want to know:
    Why does it rain, and what makes it snow?
    Why are there rivers, and where do they go?
    What are trees made of, and what makes them grow?
Thank you, God, for encyclopaedias and other books which help us to find the answers to our questions.

Home and family

Homes and houses

107 *Many different homes*
Thank you, God, for giving us homes to live in.
All over the world, people live in different sorts of homes:
    igloos made of ice, and huts of wood and mud;
    houses roofed with leaves, and houses up on stilts; sky-
    scraping flats, and low-doored cottages;
    tents made from skins, and homes on boats.
Thank you, God, for our homes.

108 *Building houses*
Introduce this prayer by talking about a local building site.
Lord, it's exciting to watch houses being built.
We see the diggers and cranes
    and cement mixers working.
We watch the walls grow higher
    and see the windows like empty eyes.
We see the builders carrying bricks, climbing ladders,
    clambering over the roof.
They are all so busy.
Keep them safe, and help them do their work well.

109 *Our homes*
Loving God, thank you for our homes
where we feel warm and safe;
where we share with our families and friends;
where we play and laugh together.
Let everyone in our home be happy,
and make everyone who comes to visit us happy too.

110 *Homeless people*
God who loves us, please help all the people in the world
who have no real homes to live in.
We pray for those who live in hostels, camps or on the
streets. Help them to find answers to their problems.
We pray, too, for those who help the homeless and
refugees. Make them loving and patient.

111 *Decorating our homes*
What a dreadful mess there is when rooms at home are
being decorated! Strips of old wallpaper on the floor, and
splashes of paint everywhere. But how lovely it is when
everything has been cleaned up, and walls and ceilings
and doors are clean and fresh. Thank you, loving God, for
our colourful homes.

112 *Warm homes*
Lord, when it is cold outside and the days are dark, it is
good to be inside our warm homes, safe from the wind,
rain and snow.
Thank you for the people who bring us coal and oil, or
provide the gas and electricity to heat our homes.
Thank you for those who take care of us and work to keep
our homes warm and cosy for us.

113 *Coming home*
Home is the place we come to
when we are tired and want to rest,

when we have some good news to share,
when we are sad and alone.
Home is the place where the people who love us are
always glad to see us.
Thank you, God, for our homes and families.

114 *Jesus' home and family*
Lord Jesus,
you lived at Nazareth in a house with a flat roof;
you listened to the Bible stories your mother, Mary,
told you;
you watched Joseph working in his carpenter's shop;
you played with your brothers and sisters.
Lord Jesus, we are glad you had a home and family, as we
do.
Help us to remember that you are always with us.

Families

115 *Love makes happy families*
What makes happy families?
Love does.
What makes families who laugh together?
Love does.
What makes families who care about each other?
Love does.
What makes families who talk and play together?
Love does.
Thank you, loving God, for happy families.

116 *Mums and dads*
*Adapt the people mentioned in this prayer to suit the
circumstances of the children with whom it is prayed.*
Mums and dads are the people
who love us and look after us;
who understand when we say, 'Sorry';
who play with us and tell us stories;
who hold our hands when we are frightened

and make us smile when we are sad.
Thank you, Lord, for our mums and dads.

117 *Brothers and sisters*
Lord, we are glad we have brothers and sisters.
We can play together, and help each other.
When we say hurtful things, help us to say, 'Sorry'.
When we disagree, help us to be friends.
When we want to keep things all to ourselves, help us
    to share.

118 *Grandparents*
Loving God, thank you for grandparents –
    for grannies and grandads, grandpas and nannas
    (add any particular names used by the children).
Some of us see our grandparents a lot – they live near us
    and help look after us.
Some of us go to stay with our grandparents or they come
    to visit us and we do special things with them.
Loving God, please take care of our grandparents, and
    help us to find ways of showing how much we love
    them.

119 *Orphaned children*
Father God, we are sad that so many children in the world
have no proper homes and no mothers and fathers of their
own, because there is fighting in their countries, or
because they are poor, hungry and ill. Loving God, give
those children people to love them and families to care for
them. Let them know that you love them.

120 *Family parties*
Talk about parties, and how Jesus liked them.
Lord Jesus, we are glad that you enjoyed parties.
We love the times when our families:
    brothers and sisters,
    parents and grandparents,
    aunts and uncles and cousins,

all get together for a family party.
Thank you for the good times we have,
for games and food and presents.
Help us to remember that you are part of our family, and
 are with us at our parties.

121 *Family friends*
Thank you, Lord, for the times when other families come to
visit us, or we visit them. The grown-ups talk together, the
children play together, we show each other our homes.
Lord, it is good to be able to share our homes.
Thank you for our family friends.

Family activities

122 *Family outings*
Loving God,
  thank you for family outings
  when we all go out together:
    for a picnic,
    or to the pantomime,
    or to the seaside or the zoo.
*(Encourage the children to suggest other places and
include them in the prayer.)*
We are glad we can go together.
It would not be so much fun on our own.
Please help lonely people to find friends to do things with
  and help us to look out for anyone who is lonely.

123 *Sharing*
Lord Jesus, sometimes we get cross:
  when someone else plays with our toys,
  or when others want to watch a different television
    programme to us,
  or *(use the children's own suggestions).*
Help us to share, and forgive us when we are unkind
  because others will not share with us.

124 *Working together*
Talk about times when everyone helps, for example to get ready for a holiday: someone packs the cases, someone else puts them in the car, children carry smaller items.

Lord, we can do things so much more quickly and easily when we all work together. Help us to work together in our families.

125 *Helping at home*
Loving God, there are so many things to do at home...
    (use suggestions from the children).
Help us not to leave the jobs for just one person to do, but
    to share the work so that no one gets too tired and
    everyone has some time to do what they want.

126 *Cooking*
Talk with the children about the ways they help with cooking and baking.

Lord Jesus, it is fun to help make meals.
    We like to chop vegetables and grate cheese *(include
    other suggestions from the children).*
    We like to weigh and measure.
    We like stirring the cake mixture (and scraping the bowl
    at the end!).
Thank you, Lord, for the lovely smell of fresh baking and
    for all the food that we enjoy.

127 *Making and mending*
Thank you, God, for our mums and dads and other people
    who help us by making and mending things for us.
    When a button falls off our clothes they sew it on.
    They patch our torn jeans.
    They fix our broken toys.
(Add the children's own ideas)
We are glad they are always there to help us.

128 *Shopping*
Loving God, we like to push the shopping trolley when we go to the supermarket.
All around are shelves full of things to eat: piles of tins and boxes of all sizes and colours. There are cheese and bread, fish and meat, apples, oranges and bananas, butter and milk and cereals.
Thank you, God, for so many good things to eat.
Help us to remember that there are many hungry people in the world who only have rice or bread to eat each day.
We pray that everyone who can will work to help change the world so that hungry people have enough to eat.

129 *Toys and hobbies*
Talk with the children about the toys they have, and hobbies they enjoy. Then ask those children who are willing to take part to say a sentence each:
Thank you, Lord, for...
Conclude.
Thank you, Lord, for toys and games, puzzles and books, and all the things we enjoy doing and playing.

130 *Illness*
Particularly suitable when a child is known to be in hospital or ill at home.
We do not like it, Lord,
    when we are ill and have to stay at home in bed;
    when we feel shaky, and stuffy with a cold.
We thank you, Lord, for people who look after us
    and make us feel well again.
Please help all children who are ill *(especially...)* and those
    who are in hospital *(especially...)*
Please make them well again soon.

Home and family

131 *Meal-times*
For tasty food when we are hungry,
for the people who worked to grow it,
for those who made and cooked it,
for those with whom we share it,
and for you, Creator God, who gave it:
  we say a special 'Thank you'.

132 *Bedtime*
Lord Jesus, I'm so very tired;
it's been a busy day.
Safe and warm in this cosy bed,
I've just two things to say:
'Sorry for wrong things which I've done –
I'll try to put them right'
and, 'Thank you for another day.'
Lord, keep me safe tonight.

Learning and playing

Nurseries, schools and playgroups

133 Praise to God for writing, reading,
teachers helping, guiding, leading.
Praise God for nurseries, schools and playgroups.
Praise to God, our Lord.

Praise to God for counting, cooking,
drawing, dancing, listening, looking.
Praise God for nurseries, schools and playgroups.
Praise to God, our Lord.

Praise to God for tapes and talking,
playing house and going walking.
Praise God for nurseries, schools and playgroups.
Praise to God, our Lord.

Praise to God for adults caring,
friends and finger-plays and sharing.
Praise God for nurseries, schools and playgroups.
Praise to God, our Lord.

134 We love you, God.
You are so good to us.
You are always there –
in the classroom,
in the playground,

in the street,
at home.
We love you, God.
You are so good to us.
You are always there –
to help us,
to keep us company,
for us to talk to,
to enjoy things with us.

135 Lord God, we want to do our best at school,
but sometimes we do not try hard enough.
We are sorry. Please help us to learn from our mistakes
and not give up.

136 Sometimes, God, we're not very good.
Sometimes we don't do the things that we should.
Sometimes we're horrid to people in school.
We're sorry, loving God.
Sometimes, God, we have a bad day.
Sometimes we want things all our own way.
Sometimes we're cross in the things that we say.
We're sorry, loving God.

137 Lord Jesus,
you told us to love one another.
Please help us to do this.
Show us how to be friends with anyone who is lonely.
Show us how to talk to anyone who is unhappy.
Show us how to smile and cheer someone up.
Please help us, Lord.

138 We are sorry, God,
for the things that we do wrong.
Sometimes we know what we ought to do,
but we do not do it.
Please help us to do better.

139 Loving God, thank you for all the places where we meet
other people and learn and play with them:
    playgroup, nursery and school,
    after-school clubs and holiday playschemes,
    childminders' and friends' houses and our own homes.
For the many different groups we belong to, we thank you,
    Lord.

140 *Talk with the children about the things they do in school,*
nursery or playgroup. Use the following prayer as a basis
for thanksgiving, but include the children's suggestions too.

For all the good things we do in school/nursery/playgroup:
    We thank you, loving God.
For sand and water play,
for sticking and making things:
    We thank you, loving God.
For painting and drawing,
for cutting out and tracing:
    We thank you, loving God.
For story-books and picture books,
for storytime and learning to read:
    We thank you, loving God.
For music and dancing,
for songs to sing and instruments to play:
    We thank you, loving God.
For counting and number games,
for poetry and finger-plays:
    We thank you, loving God.
For pictures on the walls,
for flowers and growing plants,
    We thank you, loving God.

141 Thank you, God, for swings and sand,
pictures, plays, percussion band.
Thank you, God, for pets to feed,
time to paint and time to read.

Thank you, God, for time to talk,
time to sit and time to walk.

Learning and playing

Thank you, God, for time to trace,
time to rest and time to race.

Thank you, God, for plants to grow,
bricks to build and balls to throw.
Thank you, God, for cakes to cook,
time to listen, time to look.

142 Thank you, God, that wherever we are we can learn.
At home or at school we can think and wonder, ask
questions and puzzle things out for ourselves.
Thank you that we can go on learning new things whatever
age we are.
Thank you that there is always more to discover!

143 *For use following the discovery that children in some parts
of the world may not have schools to go to.*

Loving God, we have learned that children in some
countries have no schools to go to.
We have schools with teachers and books, paints and
crayons and lots of other equipment.
We want all children to have things to write and draw with,
books to read and teachers to help them.
Please show us how we can help to make this happen.

Friends and playing

144 Loving God, we like having friends.
It would make us very sad if no one wanted to be our
friend.
Thank you for the friends we have.
Help us to notice anyone on their own, to talk to them and
ask them to join in our games.

145 Friends to play with,
friends to work with,
friends to talk with,
friends to laugh with:
thank you, God, for friends.

Friends that we can help,
friends that we can talk to,
friends to share with,
friends to be quiet with:
help us, God, to be good friends.

146 Lord, help us to be friendly to everyone, even those people
we find it difficult to like.
If anyone hurts us, or says bad things to us, help us not to
do the same back to them.
It's hard, Lord, but that is what you explained to us: we
must keep on being kind to others, even when they are not
kind to us.

147 Good friends,
kind friends,
loving friends,
helpful friends.

Friends at school,
friends at church,
friends at home,
friends on holiday.
Thank you, God, for friends

148 *Talk with the children about friendship. Ask them where
they have friends. Explain that in the prayer each of them
is to think 'inside their heads' but not to speak out loud.*

Let's be quiet and think of our friends at home. Say 'thank
you' for them and ask God to help you to be kind and
loving to each other.
Short silence
Thank you, God, for listening to us.

Let's be quiet and think of our friends at school. Say 'thank
you' for them and ask God to help you to be kind and
loving to each other.
Short silence
Thank you, God, for listening to us.

Learning and playing

Let's be quiet and think of our friends at church. Say 'thank you' for them and ask God to help you to be kind and loving to each other.

Short silence

Thank you, God, for listening to us.

(Add similar prayers about friends in any other places the children mentioned in the initial conversation.)

The Church family

Groups meeting at church

149 Here we are at church, God,
thanking you for all your love to us.
We have come with our families and friends
to bring our love to you.
Thank you for this church in which
we sing our songs of praise,
learn about your care for us,
and ask you to be with us every day.
Help us to grow together like one big family
in which everyone is wanted and loved.

150 Here we are with our friends, God, to say 'thank you' for
our church.
Please listen to the songs we sing and help us to learn
more about Jesus.

151 There are many people who help us to say our prayers
and sing our songs.
Thank you, God, for our minister, for our leaders and
helpers, for those who help us to make music.
May we all do what we can to make our church a happy
place.

152 For singing and music,
for stories and pictures,
for happy times together here in church:
thank you, loving God.

153 God, when we come to church there are many things
which help us to know and love you.

Sometimes we look at a picture which shows your
wonderful world.
(Show a suitable picture)

We listen to music which helps us to be quiet and to think
about you.
(Play a short piece of quiet music)

We hear a story from the Bible which tells of your love for
us.
*(Open the Bible at a picture of a story the children
know well)*

And we join together to sing our songs of praise.
(Sing something appropriate)

Thank you, God, for all that helps us know and love you.

154 Loving God, we are going to listen to a story *(about Jesus,
or, which Jesus told, or...)*
Bless our leader who tells it, and us as we listen.
Through the story may we find out more about you.
(Tell the story)
Thank you, loving God, for that story. There are so many
things to discover about you.
You love us so much; may we love you more and more.

155 God, we welcome new boys and girls to our church/group
today.
Welcome to ... and...
May they be happy with us, and may we all be friends of
one another and of Jesus, the friend of all.

156 Loving God,
we are glad to welcome new friends today.
Please bless them,
and help us to grow up together
loving you and loving one another.

157 Lord Jesus, you grew up as a boy at Nazareth:
you went to school and learned your lessons.
Every day we are growing up:
some of our friends are moving to another group today:
bless them and keep them,
help them and us to grow up wise and strong,
loving and following you.

158 God, thank you for our group here at church;
for ways in which we come to know more about you:
for stories, and games, for singing and playing.
Help us all to know you more,
to love you more,
and to follow you day by day.

159 It's fun being together when we go
on outings with our friends.
Bless us when we go on our church outing next...
Let it be a good time for all of us.

160 It's fun being together when we go
on outings with our friends.
Thank you, God, for the fun we had with our church
friends last...

161 God, there are so many things to discover here in church:
beautiful flowers,
smooth shiny wood,
pictures and banners,
light and patterns,

careful needlework...
(add other items as appropriate to your building).
Thank you, God, for those who look after the lovely things
in church so that we can enjoy them.
May all of us help to care for them too, so that everyone
who comes into this church can be happy here and
praise you.

162 Loving God, it is time to go home.
Thank you for our time together here at church.
Bless our homes and be with us every day.

163 We have been together here at church
and now we are going home.
For all your love,
here and wherever we are,
thank you, God.

164 Loving God,
be with us through every day of this week.
Keep us in your love until we come together at church
again.

Baptisms

165 Lord Jesus, bless the babies that have come to our church
today.
Keep them always in your love and may they grow up
loving you.

166 Jesus, you welcomed the children long ago:
bless the baby we welcome today into the family of your
church.
May he/she grow to know you and love you, day by day.

167 Jesus, we are welcoming ... *(name of child)* today.
He/she is part of your family here at our church.
Bless him/her today and every day with your love.

Harvest festival

168
Thank you, God, for all the gifts of harvest:
    fruit and flowers,
    vegetables, and other good things to eat.
May we never waste your gifts,
    but always use them wisely and well,
    sharing with those who do not have as much as we do:
for Jesus' sake.

169
Ripe red apples!
Rough brown potatoes!
Green cabbage and runner beans!
Purple and yellow plums!
Black coal and clear water!
So many colours; so many tastes!
    Thank you, God, for harvest.

170
Dear God, all around us there are the colours and smells
and tastes of your harvest gifts.
We, who have so much to thank you for, pray for those in
your world who are hungry. Show us how we can share so
that no one will be hungry or unloved.

171
We have lovely flowers in our room today:
we can enjoy their colour and scent.
They remind us that you care for your world, God,
and we know that you take care of us too.

172
Thank you, Creator God,
    for farmers who grow the food we need.
Thank you for the people who load it onto lorries and
    trailers and trains.
Thank you for shop assistants who sell us our food.
Thank you for those who prepare it and cook it.
For all these people, thank you, Creator God.

173 Eggs and apples and tins of beans are here,
with marrows and tea and flowers.
We feast on the picture they make –
the shapes, the colours, the scents.
Gladly we've given
    from our garden plots
    or well-stocked cupboard shelves,
    because we want to share.
We remember that long ago there was a boy
    who gave Jesus his loaves and fishes,
    to share with a crowd of hungry people.
Thank you, God, that we have enough to share with
    others.

Mothering Sunday

174 We are glad, God, that when Jesus came to earth he had
Mary for his mother.
She loved him and cared for him, and he loved her too.
Thank you for our mums:
    for the way they care for us.
    May we always love them.
Bless our mums today and every day.

175 Loving God, we think today about our mums.
Thank you for all they do for us and with us.
Bless them and keep them always in your love.

176 Lord, mothers are very special to us:
they care for us and teach us the way to live.
Your Church is like a mother to us, too.
Thank you for all the love and care our mothers give us,
    and for the love and care we find at church.

Church unity

177 Lord, we are all part of your Church –
    girls and boys,
    men and women,

mums, dads, aunties, uncles,
friends and neighbours.
We all belong to you and you love us all.

178 Dear God, those of us who are young ask you to bless
those in our church who are older.
May we all join to praise you for all your love which you
have shown to us in Jesus Christ.

179 We are all different, Lord,
some short, some tall;
some with curly hair, some with straight;
some with glasses;
some with teeth missing;
some with pale skin, some with dark.
We are all different, Lord, but we are all part of your family,
and we thank you that you love us all.

The Church's birthday and our birthdays

Pentecost

180
Lord Jesus,
when you went away your friends were sad.
So they started to meet together,
    to remember you and talk about you,
    to sing hymns and say prayers,
    just as we do in church.
Thank you, Lord Jesus, that we can be your friends too,
    and meet together in church.
Thank you for listening to our hymns and our prayers.
Thank you for loving us so much and never being far away.

181
Loving God,
we like to feel the wind on our faces
and watch it rustling the leaves on the trees.
We cannot see the wind, but we know it is there.
Loving God,
we like to feel happy in church
and see the smiles on our friends' faces.
We cannot see your Spirit but the Spirit is there.
Thank you for filling us with your Holy Spirit and giving us
so much happiness.

182 Lord, help us, your Church family, to remember how you
want us to live.
Like the first Christians, help us to be friends together,
share our things, help others, and pray together.
In that way we can carry on the work of the first Church,
and live as Jesus wants us to live.

183 *Let the children pretend to be the flames of a fire leaping
up and down, and then in sharp contrast to behave like a
gentle breeze, swaying from side to side. Mime the actions
to fit with the prayer.*
Let us praise God by
jumping, leaping,
dancing, shouting,
just like flames of fire.
Let us praise God by
sitting, swaying,
thinking, praying,
just like a gentle breeze.
Thank you, God, for times when our church is lively and
we can feel your power.
Thank you, God, for times when our church is quiet and
we can feel your peace.

184 When the Church began, it began with a promise, a
promise from Jesus. Jesus promised his friends that he
would still love them and help them, even though they
could not see him.
Thank you, Lord, for that marvellous promise,
because it means we can be sure of Jesus' love;
it means we can be sure that he will help us;
and most of all it means that the Church today can
grow and become more loving.

185 Let us pray for God's Church on its birthday. Let us pray
that the Church family may grow in many ways in the
coming year:

> that we may grow in love for one another,
> that we may grow in happiness,
> that we may grow and learn more about Jesus.
> Thank you for our birthday Church.

Church Anniversary

186
We are celebrating a birthday today, God:
it is the birthday of our church.
Thank you for those who built it,
for those who care for it,
and for those who join with us to show you our love.
Help us all to grow up following the ways of Jesus who is
our leader.

Birthdays

187
*To introduce this prayer, count slowly – one, two, three,
four, etc. – inviting the children to raise their hands when
they hear their age.*

We are growing up, Lord!
Birthdays mean we are one year older:
growing taller,
growing bigger,
learning new things,
making new friends.
Growing up is exciting, Lord.
Thank you for birthdays which make us happy every year.

188
Loving God, it is ...'s birthday today.
Thank you for keeping him/her safe for another year.
Help him/her to have a very happy birthday,
to enjoy his/her cards and presents,
and any special things he/she will be doing.
Thank you for all the fun we have when we share the
happiness of our friends' birthdays.

189
Lord, when our birthday arrives, we listen for the postman
coming to the door. We run to pick up all our cards, and rip

open the envelopes! It's very exciting!
Thank you for birthday cards with pictures of toys and candles and cakes.
Thank you for birthday cards with badges or balloons or gifts inside.
Most of all, thank you for the kind people who send them: people who love us so much that they want to say, 'Happy Birthday!' Thank you, Lord.

190 *Talk about parcels.*
Long ones, lumpy ones,
big ones, bumpy ones,
all shapes and sizes,
stuffed with surprises:
games and toys,
for girls and boys;
hidden away until The Day.
Thank you, Lord, for all the things
that every happy birthday brings.

191 *Talk about presents or small gifts the children may have given recently.*

Dear Jesus, we know that you want your friends to give presents, not just to get them.
So please help us to remember other people's birthdays.
We could make them a card, or a small present, or just remember to smile and say, 'Happy Birthday'.
Our birthdays are important, and so are those of other people. Help us to show others we love them.

192 Let us pray for children who do not have happy birthdays.
Please, God, bless children who live
in countries where there is not enough food,
or in homes that are cold,
or in poor families where there is not enough money for cards or presents or cakes.
Please, God, help those children to know that you love them and show us what we can do to help give them a better life.

People's jobs

193 *Talk with the children about the people who deliver things at their homes. Have a selection of suitable articles to be held up as visual aids.*

Let us think about the people who deliver things to our homes:
> the person who brings us milk *(hold up bottle/carton)*;
> the post *(hold up letters)*;
> the newspaper *(hold one up)*;
> *(add other people as suggested by the children).*

We thank you, God, for all the people who bring things to our homes.

194 For people who love us – cuddling, sharing,
cooking, cleaning, shopping, caring,
holding our hands when we cross the streets,
washing and ironing, and changing the sheets –
we thank you, loving God.

195 *Think together of those who visit our homes to do work for us, e.g. window-cleaners, painters, plumbers, electricians.*

So many people come to our homes, loving God, to help us in so many ways.

People's jobs

We are glad that there are clever people to help us care for our homes and the things in them.

196 As we look around us, Lord, we can see so many different things that people have made:
the chairs...
the table...
the curtains...
the carpet...
(add other items suggested by the children.)
Thank you, God, for the people who made all these things for us to use.

197 *Complete the second part of the prayer with appropriate local details.*

Lord, it must be fun to drive a train, or a big lorry, or a bus, or a car.
But we know it is also difficult, and dangerous, and tiring.
Lord, we think of the people who will be driving round our town today:
the train driver bringing the train from...,
the lorry drivers who bring things to our shops,
the driver of the number ... bus that passes our church/school/home,
our parents/friends who sometimes give us a lift in their car.
Keep them all safe as they travel, please, Lord.

198 We pray today for the police,
patrolling in the street,
guiding, protecting, advising,
helping all they meet.
We pray for those who sweep our roads
and clean up in the town,
collecting all the rubbish
careless folk throw down.
We pray for those who plant the flowers
that grow in every park.

We pray for those who put up lamps,
    lighting up the dark.
We pray for all who work in towns
    during day and night,
to make our roads and paths and parks
    attractive, safe and bright.

199

*Appropriate pictures of workers (verse 1) and children
(verse 2) would form a useful visual aid.*

For those who work on buses,
    and those who clean the streets,
for those who take the rubbish,
    and those who sell us sweets,
for those who tell us stories,
    and those who cook our tea,
I thank you, loving God,
    that they do these things for me.

Lord, keep us kind and thoughtful,
    and help us all to be
the kind of loving people
    you always like to see.
We'll try to be so friendly and smile at those we meet
    at home, in shops, in parks, in church,
in school and in the street.

200

*Position four children facing the rest of the group, each
holding or wearing an object to indicate a job. In turn each
child steps forward as the leader prays.*

Child holding spade or hoe
For those who dig and plant and weed,
who work outside in wind and rain and sun
to grow our food:
    We thank you, loving God.
Child holding a box or sack
For those who pack the food carefully
so that it can be carried safely to us:
    We thank you, loving God.
Child wearing sailor's hat or holding toy ship
For those who work in ships

bringing our food across the sea:
We thank you, loving God.
Child with shop assistant's overall or toy till
For those who work in shops
selling us good things to eat:
We thank you, loving God.

201 *Talk about the different shops the children know. Add more shops to the prayer, as appropriate.*

Loving God, we are glad there are so many shops, with
people ready to sell us the things we need:
    the shop/supermarket where we buy our groceries,
        and the assistants who stock up the shelves,
        and take our money at the checkout;
    the greengrocer's shop,
        and the greengrocer who goes to market very early
        to buy fresh fruit and vegetables for us;
    the shop where we buy plasters and soap and
        toothpaste, and the chemist who sells us good
        medicines;
    the shops where we buy clothes and shoes,
        and the kind assistants who help us choose them.
Loving God, thank you for people who work in shops.

202 Loving God, we thank you for the people who make sure
we keep healthy and strong:
    the health visitors who help and advise our mums and
    dads;
    the nurses who take care of us if we go to hospital;
    the doctors who make us well again when we are ill;
    the dentists who look after our teeth.
We do not like to be ill, God. We think of people who are
ill now... Please make them patient and brave and help
them to get well soon.

203 *Talk with the children about the people who work at their school or visit it from time to time. Pray for them by name when possible. Add the children's own suggestions and* *adapt the prayer as necessary.*

For the teachers who help us to do so many exciting and interesting things at school:
>**Thank you, God.**

For the caretaker and cleaners who keep our school tidy and clean and warm:
>**Thank you, God.**

For the people who work in the kitchens to make tasty meals for us, and wash up afterwards:
>**Thank you, God.**

For the gardeners who cut the grass and look after the grounds:
>**Thank you, God.**

For the nurse who comes to make sure we are well:
>**Thank you, God.**

For the dentist who comes to look at our teeth:
>**Thank you, God.**

For the person who comes to talk to us about how to cross the road safely:
>**Thank you, God.**

For the person from the library who comes to show us books:
>**Thank you, God.**

204 Loving God, we like to go to the library to borrow books. Sometimes we can listen to story hour there.
Thank you for the authors who write the stories and for the artists who draw the pictures.
Thank you for the librarian who helps us to choose books and stamps them with the date.
Help us to take care of the books we borrow, so that other people may enjoy them too.

205 Loving God, we like to go to the swimming pool.
Thank you for the people who work there:
the person who takes our money,
the instructor who shows us what to do,
the attendant who makes sure we are safe.

Please, God, help us to be sensible in the water and in the changing room so that we can all enjoy ourselves safely.

206 *Talk with the children about their special interests which include instruction, e.g. having dancing or music lessons. Adapt the prayer according to the interest being thought about. Mention people by name when possible.*

Loving God, we like to go to *dancing lessons*.
Thank you for the people who help us:
    ... who teaches us,
    ... who plays the piano,
    ... who helps us change.
Loving God, help us to be cheerful and helpful, so that children and adults can have a happy time.

207 *Talk with the children about their favourite television programmes, and favourite television presenters and characters. Include the appropriate programmes and people in the prayer.*

Lord God, we like watching television.
We like ... *(names of programmes)* and ... *(names of presenters)*.
Thank you for the fun of watching television.
We think of the people who work hard to bring the television pictures to us:
    writers and artists,
    camera crews and sound recordists,
    directors and producers,
    actors and actresses.
Thank you for the fun of watching television.

208 Thank you, God, for music:
    music for dancing;
    music for marching;
    music that makes us want to tap our feet;
    music for listening to quietly;
    music that makes us feel lively and excited;
    music that helps us to praise you.
Thank you, God, for music and the people who make it.

209 Loving God, thank you for television and radio programmes, for videos, tapes and CDs. Thank you for the programmes, the stories and music we see and hear, and for all the people who work hard to make it possible for us to enjoy them.

210 *Use parts of the prayer as appropriate. Other occupations can be thought of and similar prayers prepared and used.*

Dear God, there are many people who work to provide us with things we need. Today we think of some of them.

Thank you for the farmer who grows corn,
and for the miller who grinds it into flour,
and for the baker who makes flour into bread and cakes.
Please be with them in their work.

Thank you for market-gardeners who grow vegetables:
working outside in all weathers,
sowing, weeding, spraying, watering, hoeing,
harvesting the crops and packing them.
Please be with them in their work.

Thank you for dairy farmers who keep cows:
they have to keep the stalls clean,
and provide hay for the cattle in winter,
and milk them every day.
Please be with them in their work.

Thank you for dairy workers
who turn milk into cream and butter,
yoghurt and cheese, for us to enjoy;
they have to work carefully and cleanly.
Please be with them in their work.

Thank you for people who fish the seas in cold and storm:
their work is often dangerous and difficult,
as they bring their catch to a safe harbour.
Please be with them in their work.

Thank you for coal-miners and oil workers,
gas and power-station workers:
their work is often hard or dirty or dangerous;
we are glad of the fuel they supply
for warmth and light and cooking.
Please be with them in their work.

People's jobs

Thank you for factory workers
who make so many things we use:
bikes and toys,
paper and books,
shoes and clothes,
furniture, curtains and carpets
(add other things suggested by the children).
Please be with them in their work.
Thank you for people who build houses and flats
for us to live in:
architects and surveyors,
bricklayers and carpenters,
roofers and plasterers,
electricians and plumbers,
decorators and painters;
all have their work to do.
Please be with them in their work.
Thank you for people who help in emergencies:
the fire-brigade who rush to put out burning buildings,
or to help free people and animals who get stuck;
ambulance drivers who take people to hospital,
speeding safely through the traffic;
the police who help when there has been an accident,
making the roads safe again for travellers;
(use the children's own ideas).
Please be with them in their work.

211 *Following an outing, discuss with the children all that they
enjoyed, and mention the people who worked to make it
possible. Adapt the prayer as necessary.*

Lord God, we enjoyed the day we went to... Thank you for
the people who worked so hard to make it possible for us:
for ... who drove the minibus,
for ... who made our packed lunches,
for ... who sold us tickets at the gate,
for ... who told us so many interesting things,
for ... who helped when...
Thank you, God, for the kind people in your world.

Holidays, outings and games

Holidays

212 Thank you, God, that every day is not the same.
Thank you for holidays when we can do different things:
    going on outings;
    visiting friends and relations;
    joining a playscheme;
    playing with our toys at home and in the garden.
Thank you, God, for holidays.

213 Holidays are fun!
There are so many things to enjoy.
    We enjoy the feeling of sand between our toes, and
      water tickling our feet;
    we enjoy the taste of ice-cream and chocolate, and
      new, exciting foods;
    we enjoy seeing new places, and meeting different
      people;
    we enjoy the sounds of the seaside: waves breaking,
      seagulls crying, ships hooting,
    and of the countryside: cows lowing, sheep bleating,
      the roar of farm machinery and tractors;
    we enjoy the smell of salt in the wind and the scent of
      wild flowers and grass.
Loving God, thank you for holidays.

Holidays, outings and games

214
Thank you, God, for the seaside:
    for the sandy beach and the splashing waves,
    for sand-castles and seaweed,
    for crabs and shells and rocks.
You made them all and we enjoy them.
Thank you.

215
Talk with the children about holidays they remember.
Sometimes we go away for holidays,
sometimes we stay at home.
Sometimes we camp in a tent or caravan.
Sometimes we go abroad, by plane or train or ferry.
Wherever we go, we enjoy seeing new things and having
    fun.
Thank you, God, for holidays.

216
Summer holidays mean
    hearing the birds sing in the early morning,
    going out for the day,
    hot sun and picnics,
    or getting wet in the rain,
    swimming and paddling,
    treats and ice-creams,
    sand-castles and fun fairs,
    often going to bed late.
Thank you for holidays, God, and for friends and family to
share them with.

217
*Talk about people the children have visited. Recall their
names and what they did together.*
Loving God, we thank you for giving us friends and
relations to visit.
We think especially of...
Thank you for the fun we had when...
    Please bless them all. Keep them happy together.
    May everyone who visits their homes be happy too.

218
For outings in the car
in many kinds of weather,
with adults, children, toys and pets
all snuggled in together,
  we thank you, loving God.
For family picnics on the grass,
and playing in the sun,
for sandwiches and crisps and sweets,
and lots and lots of fun,
  we thank you, loving God.

Travelling

219
Talk with the children about journeys they have made and different kinds of transport.
Loving God, there are so many ways to get from place to place:
    by train – overground or underground,
    by buses, coaches, cars and trams,
    by boats and planes,
    and on our own two feet!
Thank you, God, for so many ways to travel.

220
Dear loving God, sometimes we travel by bus.
We wait at the bus stop until the bus comes.
Then we climb aboard and give our money to the driver or
    conductor.
We choose our seats, and watch the other people on the
    bus or look out of the window.
When we reach our stop, we get off carefully, and wave
    goodbye to the driver.
It's fun to travel by bus.
Thank you for bus journeys.
Please bless all those who work on the buses, and those
    who travel on them.

Holidays, outings and games

Outings

221 *Following a visit to a wood or forest, look together at fircones, leaves, grass, acorns and so on.*

Thank you, God, for the forest:
    tall fir trees with long straight trunks,
    leafy oak trees with strong, spreading branches...
    (add any special trees noticed).
Thank you, God, for many kinds of leaves:
    dark green and light green,
    pointed and rounded, smooth and rough.
Thank you, God, for seeds in the forest:
    chestnuts and acorns, fir cones and...
    (add any others found).
Thank you, God, for animals in the forest:
    ponies and deer, foxes, squirrels and...
    (add any others seen).
Thank you, God, for birds that nest in the trees and sing in
    the branches:
    (name any seen and known).
Loving God, the forest is very beautiful.
Help us to keep it beautiful for others to enjoy.

222 *Recall a visit to a zoo, and encourage the children to add the creatures they remember seeing.*

Dear Lord, how many creatures you have made!
We saw lions and tigers,
    elephants and camels,
    zebras and kangaroos,
    monkeys and bears, and...
Dear Lord, how many birds you have made!
We saw large ones and small ones,
    brown ones and brightly-coloured ones,
    birds with long legs and beaks,
    birds with strong wings and claws, and...
Thank you, Lord, for making so many living creatures.
Thank you for making us, too.

223 Loving God, when the sun shines and it is warm outside we like to play games in the garden or park. We like skipping and ball games, playing chase and hide-and-seek, soaring high on the swings, swooping down the slide... *(add the children's own suggestions).*
Thank you, God, for gardens and parks to play in and friends to play with.

Activities and games

224 Loving God, we enjoy pretending to be other people:
  mums and dads and babies,
  shopkeepers, racing car drivers and footballers
  (add other suggestions from the children).
Thank you for our imaginations and the fun of pretending.

225 Creator God, when we paint pictures we use brushes and paper and many different colours.
Thank you for beautiful colours and interesting shapes.
Thank you for giving us hands to use for painting, and eyes to see our pictures.

226 Dear Lord, we like playing with a doll's house, and all the things that fit inside:
  tables and chairs,
  beds and cupboards,
  saucepans and plates,
  and... *(use the children 's suggestions).*
When we grow up, we hope to have homes of our own.
Help us, as we grow, to learn to look after our homes.

227 Dear Lord, we can make all sorts of things with building bricks:
  houses, farms and factories,
  boats and cars,
  castles, towers and bridges.
It's fun inventing and making things.
Thank you for our hands, our eyes and our imaginations.

Holidays, outings and games

228 Loving God, we have had such fun with the dough/clay/plasticene today!
  We have rolled it and squeezed it,
  pinched it and pulled it,
  cut it and pressed it.
We have made so many things:
  people and animals,
  fruit and vegetables,
  cakes and biscuits...
  (add other items/adapt as appropriate).
Best of all we liked making...
Thank you, God, for the fun of working with dough/clay/plasticene.

229 Loving God, we love to run and jump.
Thank you for:
  races in the park;
  splashing through puddles;
  scrunching our way through autumn leaves.
Thank you for:
  balls to kick and throw;
  swings and climbing frames and slides;
  and quiet cuddles at the end of a tiring day!

230 Dear Lord, thank you for bikes.
  We can ride them round the garden, and along the path.
  We can ride them to the shops and help carry the shopping home.
  We can ride to the park and to visit friends.
Thank you for legs to pedal with, for hands to steer with
  and eyes to see where we are going.
Help us not to bump into other people or to hurt them
  when we are riding.
Dear Lord, thank you for our bikes.

231 Lord, we like to play games, all together.
We play card games and word games,
  building games and ball games,
  board games with dice and counters,
  and... *(use the children's suggestions)*.
Thank you for the laughter we have together.
We are sorry for the times when we get cross because we
  have not won.
Help us always to enjoy games, whether we win or not.

232 Loving God, we hear all kinds of music:
  happy songs and sad songs,
  loud music and soft music,
  the noisy sound of loud trumpets,
  and gentle sounds that send us to sleep.
We can sing songs, or clap to their tunes,
we can move and dance to music.
We can hear different musical instruments:
  pianos and guitars, flutes and recorders,
  violins and drums...
(add the children's suggestions).
We can play CDs, tapes and records
  and listen to music on the radio.
We thank you for all these different kinds of music,
  and for the hymns and songs we learn and sing at
  church.
Thank you, God, for music.

The seasons

233 *Talk with the children about the weather. Set the weather chart. Choose the appropriate seasonal prayer.*

It's springtime, God!
Thank you for all the signs of life:
    bulbs sprouting from the ground,
    buds on the trees,
    and new-born animals.
It's springtime – **hurray!**

Summer has come!
Thank you, God, for the long, warm days of summer.
    We begin to think about holidays,
    going for walks,
    swimming and playing.
It's summer – **hurray!**

The leaves on the trees are turning brown and red and yellow.
Thank you for the autumn, God:
    for the lovely smells and wonderful colours,
    for all the harvest richness.
It's autumn – **hurray!**

Winter has come.
    Everything seems to be asleep;
    the days are dark and cold,

but we know that everything is being made ready for
the springtime.
Thank you, God, for winter:
for snow and rain and wind
which make your world ready for the coming spring.
It's winter – **hurray!**

Spring

234 *Spring in the country*
As March winds blow, the blackthorn bushes bloom,
   and tell us spring is here.
New buds appear along the hedge,
   with signs of new green leaves.
In the rough grass we see pale primroses – brand new!
We search for violets by the sunlit path,
   and then reach up to touch fluffy pussy willow and
   yellow catkins.
Quite soon, in nearby gardens, we'll see the cherry trees
   laden with white blossom, and new pink buds on apple
   trees .
How glad we are for signs of new life, God!
How glad we are to welcome spring!

235 *Spring in the town*
In town, just now, the square is bright with daffodils – big
   and yellow with golden trumpets. They make us smile
   and think of springtime.
The roundabout is carpeted with crocuses – purple and
   stripy-white.
From the bus window we see the sticky buds bursting and
   crumpled baby leaves peeping out.
As we walk along the pavement, we see brave young
   weeds pushing up between the slabs.
The winter's rest is over. It's wake-up time!
Thank you, God, for new life in all your world.

236 *Rainbow and showers*
The sun is shining, washing's on the line, children are at
   play. Drops of rain, then more – a shower!

Children shriek! Clothes pegs fly, sheets are gathered in a
  heap.
A smiling sun peeps round the cloud – waiting to play the
  game again!
Sun-rays mingle with the rain, and a rainbow arches, high
  in the sky. This is God's multi-coloured promise of love.
We praise and thank you, Creator God, for sun and
  shower and rainbow.

237 *Bird song and nests*
Very early every morning the birds wake up and sing,
'Spring, spring, spring, spring is here'.
We see them gather twigs and straw to build their nests,
    high in the hedge, or in the garden shed.
Each woven cup, all softly lined with moss,
    will make a home for baby birds, in time.
When eggs are laid, loud sing the birds!
Proudly, they tell the world.
    Loving God, we know that you care for every bird, and
    love to hear their songs. Help us to care for them too,
    and love them as you do.

238 *Planting seeds*
*Have available one or more packets of seeds. At
appropriate points in the prayer, shake the packet, then
open it and distribute the seeds to the children.*

Seed packets, all brightly coloured, show the flowers that
will grow. Listen as we shake them.
Some seeds are large and knobbly brown, and some are
very small.
With care we'll plant them in the ground or in a window
box. We'll water them, and then we'll wait.
Dear Lord, it's very hard to wait: we long to see the flowers
now. Help us to watch and care as the young plants grow.
Help us to wait patiently for the flowers that will come.

239 *Lambs*
Thank you, God, for spring's new life.

Soft woolly lambs, all legs and tails:
  we love to stand and watch.
We love to see their bouncy play,
  and listen to their calls.
Dear God, they are so glad to be alive!
Help us to be joyful like them.

240 *Frog-spawn*
God, you make us curious
about how creatures come to life,
so you have made the frogs lay eggs
 that everyone can see.
We watch each small black spot swell, and jerk, and grow.
It eats away the jellied mass until a tadpole wriggles free.
We watch legs grow, and tail disappear,
until at last we see – a tiny frog!
A miracle of life! Praise be!
  Praise to you, 0 God, for all new life.

241 *Baby animals*
Let's close our eyes and imagine –
  a day-old chick in our hands:
  so light, and soft, and chirpy.
Let's close our eyes and imagine –
  a baby rabbit in our hands,
  with furry coat and silken ears.
Let's close our eyes and imagine –
  a kitten small in our hands,
  with pretty face, and tail, and tiny claws.
Thank you, God, for all new life.
Help us to watch, and feel, and listen.
Help us to be gentle and loving with all young creatures.

Summer

242 *By the river*
Laughing and shouting we run to the river.
Are the ducks about today?
Let's throw in some pebbles and watch the splashes.
What fun!
We lie on our tummies and stir the water with a stick.
Can you see any fish, beetles, or watery worms?
A moorhen scurries on the opposite bank,
and out from the reeds comes a mother duck,
leading her young.
Move softly and slowly to offer your crumbs;
is she sure you mean her no harm?
Dear God, we're sorry when we frighten your creatures.
Teach us to understand how to make friends with them.

243 *Sounds of a summer evening*
After tea we go out to play
and listen for the chimes of the ice-cream van.
As we sit on the wall or play in the trees,
we can hear the buzz of honey bees.
We're called indoors – it's time for bed.
The blackbird sings an evening song.
Heads on our pillows, the last thing we hear
is the neighbourly mowers that clatter and whine.
For the special sounds of summer time, thank you, God.

244 *Sun*
Thank you, God, for the big, round sun.
We like to feel its warmth.
We like to see it shining on the lake or sea –
making water sparkle and dance.
We like to see the patterns it makes on the ground
when it shines through the trees.
When we feel sad, it helps us to smile again.
Lord, help us to be like sunshine to people we meet.

245 *Young birds*
Some baby birds sit in the tree
    making a terrible din!
It's time to learn to fly!
Their parents fuss and flutter round
    showing them what to do,
till one at a time the young ones fall
    or fly
      down,
        down to the ground.
Young starlings strutting on the lawn
    squawk and open their beaks,
    hoping to be fed.
But parent birds give a friendly prod
    and show them how to peck.
Day after day they do the same
    till the hungry young will try.
Dear God, we're glad that you look after birds
    and care for us as well.
You love and care for all.

246 *Dandelions*
*Put some dandelions in a jar or vase, or go outside and
look at them growing.*

Dandelions are bright – like sunshine.
We see them growing in the grass,
    or put them in a pot –
    a pot of gold?
Dandelion clocks are very soft – like fluff.
We touch them lightly with our finger tips,
    then gently blow –
    and watch each little seed parachute to earth.
Jesus said, 'Look how the wild flowers grow.
    It is God who clothes the wild grass.'
Thank you, God, for the beauty of dandelions.

247 *August storm*
God, when thunder claps we block our ears
    and feel a bit afraid.
Birds are silent. Creatures hide away.
Louder and louder the thunder sounds.
Drops of rain fall, one by one,
    until suddenly,
    hailstones bounce on the pavement,
    and rattle against the windows.
The bright lightning flashes
    and loud thunder crashes
    make us excited, God –
    but still we feel a little bit afraid.
Help us to know that you are with us.
Help us to know that the storm is part of your world, too.

248 *Cool grass*
Encourage the children to respond in movement.

Imagine you are in a park or garden on a really hot day.
You are tired, and your feet are hot and dusty.
You pull off your sandals – but oh, the path is so hot!
You jump onto the shady lawn. Cool grass!
You spread out your toes and press them deep. Soothing grass!
Down you flop and feel the coolness with your hands, your arms, your legs.
The cool grass makes you feel glad from your head to your toes.
Thank you, Lord, for cool green grass.

249 *Dragon-flies*
Playing beside the water
    we see small dragon-flies settle on the reeds,
    with see-through wings and long, slim, bright bodies.
Sometimes a big brown dragon-fly zooms by;
    first this way, then that, and back again.
    We can hear the whirr of its wings.
Thank you, God, for dragon-flies.
We wonder how such fragile wings can be so strong!

Autumn

250 *Planting bulbs for indoors*
Our hands are very dirty, God, because we're planting bulbs.
We love the feel of the damp fibre as we pack it into bowls and pots.
Help these bulbs, God, to grow into beautiful flowers, which will brighten up the lives of people who can't go outdoors.
Make them glad to see the flowers. May the beauty and the colours help them to think of you.

251 *Cobwebs*
How can spiders weave so many webs?
They look like fragile wheels
    pulled across the doorway,
    stretched over bushes,
    or gently laid upon the lawn.
But, best of all, dear God,
    we love to see them hung with dew!
    They look like diamonds, shining in the sun!
Thank you, God, for all your amazing creatures.

252 *Sunsets*
When on our way to bed we sometimes see
    bright streaks of pink and gold across the sky.
The fiery sun colours each scrap of cloud
    as it drops slowly down.
Dear God, when we see your sunset colours
    we are filled with wonder and praise!

253 *Toadstools*
With adequate supervision the children could make a toadstool 'garden' in a seed tray. Remind them never to eat any toadstools.

It's toadstool time!
Beside the road,
deep in the wood,

or on the garden lawn,
we see them:
white balls,
flat brown plates,
dainty grey parasols,
or bright red caps with spots of white!
What fun you must have had, God,
making so many, many different ones!

254

Wild fruits and nuts
*Adapt as required. Where possible, let the children handle
and taste samples. As each is mentioned in the prayer,
hold it up for the children to see.*

Let us thank our loving Father God for berries and nuts.
For tasty blackberries,
   Thank you, loving God.
For hazel-nuts to crack,
   Thank you, loving God.
For rose hips to make syrup,
   Thank you, loving God.
For chestnuts to roast,
   Thank you, loving God.
For bilberries to make pies,
   Thank you, loving God.
Thank you, loving God, for eyes to see, fingers to feel,
and tongues to taste your autumn gifts.

255

Autumn leaves
Lord, we love windy days
when the coloured leaves are tumbling:
yellow and gold, brown, bronze and red.
Laughing we race and scramble to catch them.
We scoop up armfuls of the leaves
and toss them into the wind.
They look like scraps of gold.
How much richness you have given us, loving God.

256 *Conkers*
We love conkers –
  hard and smooth and shiny,
  gleaming deep red-brown.
Dear God, our hands are piled high with them.
Thank you for this lovely treasure.

Winter

257 *Rain*
It's raining!
When we look out of the window
the people we see look sad –
  because it's raining!
Look at the drops of rain falling in the puddles.
Look at the patterns they make –
  rings and then more rings.
When we have our boots on, we jump into the puddles.
We watch the splashes we make.
We watch the water dripping from the gutters.
We listen to it gurgling down the drain.
Thank you, God, for the fun we have when it rains.

258 *The town after dark*
In town at night there are so many lights:
  the headlights of the cars and buses,
  lights in shop windows and on the street.
So many cheerful lights are round us!
Dear God, help us to be like cheerful lights so that people
who meet us are made happy.

259 *Frost and ice*
Spiky icicles hang from the shed
  like silvery swords.
Yesterday's puddles are hard to crack today.
Each wire of the fence, each twig, each blade of grass
  is white with frost,
    as though to make us notice it afresh.
Today the world looks 'special':

a special gift – with love from God!
    Thank you, God, for this special gift.

260 *Winter storms*
When the winds howl round the house, and freezing rain
beats on the windows, we're glad to be indoors.
When big trees creak and groan, and young trees bend
low, we shiver, and are glad to be indoors.
    Great Father God, we thank you for our homes.
    We thank you for our families who comfort us and make
us feel safe.
    We think of people who have no homes:
may they find shelter from the storm.

261 *Feeding the birds*
When the ground is frozen hard,
tits and robins and blackbirds, too,
are glad to come and feed.
We hang up nuts, and put out crumbs,
and lard and cheese and apple chunks – then watch!
We laugh to see tits upside-down,
pecking at the swinging nuts.
Some birds chase others away,
while some wait patiently to have their turn.
    Help us, dear God, to remember to feed the birds
till the snow and frost have gone.

262 *Footprints in the snow*
When the snow is fresh
    it's fun to be the first to make footprints,
        stride after stride.
But here and there, we see
    where birds have hopped,
        and little creatures run in search of food,
and curious cats have padded round,
    across the frozen pond.
Dear God, we thank you for footprints in the snow.

263 *Playing in the snow*
We wake in the morning to see a white world:
    Hurray!
With boots and scarves and joyful shouts,
    we're out!
The snow's so soft, so cold to taste!
With adult help, and laughs and shouts
    we make a snowman,
    with eyes of stones, and a carrot nose.
We drag a sledge to the nearest slope:
    we slide and roll,
    and our eyes water in the icy cold.
Loving God, what fun we have in the snow!
    Thank you!
Help us to remember the people for whom snow makes life
more difficult. Show us how we can help them.

264 *Evergreens*
In winter, when most trees look dead,
    we notice the evergreens.
We watch the firs bend and sway in the gale:
    their needles will not tear or be tossed away.
We watch the snow and rain slide off
    the thick, shiny leaves of other evergreens:
    they will not rot when they become wet.
Dear God, how well you have planned these trees!
We are glad that at Christmas time we choose
    a fir tree to have a special place,
    and gather holly, too.
They are part of the world that welcomes your baby Son,
Jesus.